Patty and Roy Teach You

Monsters of the Internet

Copyright © 2021 Patricia Hernández Figueroa & Rogelio E. Bernal
ALL RIGHTS RESERVED.

ISBN: 978-1-952779-98-5
Library of Congress Number: 2021908658

FIG FACTOR MEDIA

Dedication

This book is dedicated to the thousands of kids that have been victims of abuse through the different faces of the Internet. Kids and teenagers are vulnerable victims, and such abuse brings disastrous outcomes, which include traumas or suicides. They are a result of the terrible experiences caused by these hidden monsters.

Patty and Roy

Acknowledgments

Thank you to our beloved children, Julio Cesar (Pecokin), Rogelio Jr. (Papish), André (Panzón), and Savannah (Nena). To all those children that were, are, and will be under our care. To our assistants and family parents. Because you motivate us to keep doing research and finding ways to help and protect the most vulnerable individuals in our society: the children.

Patty and Roy

Welcome to the series of books
Patty and Roy Teach You

A series of books dedicated to all the little kids from anywhere in the world, in which Patty and Roy research into complicated topics and explain them to you in a fun way.

Patty and Roy invite you to join in an adventure and learn new things.

Are you ready to learn?

Dear little friend:

When we created this book, we were really worried, because we became aware that a lot of kids were victims of abuse while browsing through the Internet. We want to protect you from the monsters hidden in the Internet and teach you about the preventive measures and precautions that you must follow. In this book you will find different ways to avoid facing information that is not good for you, and you will learn how to cope with the hidden monsters.

The thing is that there are people in the digital world that wear costumes, so you see them as good people, but in fact, there are bad intentions below their masks. They want your information and your family's information. They want to use games to attract you to them. They even present really dangerous challenges and make them go viral. They want to share inappropriate pictures, and they even threat you to do what they ask you to.

To avoid being a victim of blackmail, harassment and threats, learn how to avoid and face Internet monsters.

Are you ready?

First of all, we want to you know which the risks of Internet are and how to avoid them. Internet has become an essential part of our daily lives. It is an open window to a digital world full of information that may be good or bad. We are going to tell you about some evil monsters that live in the Internet world, that want to deceive and hurt kids like you. We want you to learn how to use what you see, consciously, with responsibility and respect, and taking care of yourself.

Try to go through this window under the supervision of your parents or a close responsible adult, so they can help you discover and know about the things that you are searching and that are important to you.

We have prepared this book with love and respect. We are your friends.

Patty and Roy

THE IMPORTANT HISTORY OF THE INTERNET

Internet came to stay and it became a very important tool in our lives. Here is its history.

In 1962, the Advanced Research Projects Agency of the United States, also known as ARPA, created a computer research program, which was led by Joseph Carl Robnett Licklinder, a scientist of the MIT (Massachusetts Institute of Technology).

By 1967, enough research had been done, so the ARPA published a plan to create a computer network called ARPANET. That is to say, Internet was the result of a military project, and today, it is an essential part of our lives.

Nowadays, Internet is a network that connects with other networks and devices to share information through web pages, sites, and software.

BUT...?

There are several monsters on the Internet. They have no limits, no boundaries, and they have the power to access any kind of information. If we are not careful, they can cause us a lot of harm. This is why we talk about the seven most dangerous monsters of the Internet.

The Not for Kids Information Monster
(violence, gore images, pornography, etc.)

If this monster is near you, he may arouse very strong, negative and unknown emotions on you. For example, you may not be able to sleep or you may feel scared at night. You may be distracted during class, at home or even when you are with your friends.

You may feel really scared or terrified, want to cry or be upset or angry for no particular reason. It is possible that you do not want to eat. You may experience many negative and depressing emotions.

To avoid facing such monster, you should not visit websites that you do not know or that were not recommended by your parents.

The Contacting People with No Good Intentions Monster.

It is likely that many people send you friend requests or unknown emails through social networks. In many cases, these people's intentions are not good, even if they tell you many times that they are your friends.

Sometimes, they may even say that they know you. They will also try to find ways of fooling you to gain your trust and obtain what they want.

They may pretend to be a kid just like you. The worst thing is that there is no way to actually know it. Do not accept invitations from strangers and, if you have questions or doubts, better ask your parents. They will guide you in the best way and you will prevent this monster from entering into your life and hurting you.

The Sharing Private Information Monster

This monster is very smart, many people call him "hacker." This monster loves stealing personal information. Such piece of information is private and, in many cases, only your parents have it.

He likes creating deceptive ads and knows how to fool you to fall into their clutches. While you use your computer there may appear some sign reading: "Click here and win." Once you have entered and accepted the terms or provided any passwords of your email accounts or your parents' bank accounts, or if you have given any credit card number without your parents' consent, they will steal information.

You can prevent this cyber attack by buying only in websites authorized by your parents. Do not click on any link that you receive, even if they look fun, full of colors or offer attractive prizes. Your parents must always know!

Remember to ask before doing any action of this kind with your computer.

The Bullying or Being Bullied Monster

This monster will try to cause the highest damage possible. He works with messages containing things that you do not like, and he loves laughing at the way you look or the things you like. He draws on your pictures or adds marks to your videos as well as on any other thing you have shared. He will try to use everything to hurt you. This monster is so dangerous that is contagious and may cause that other people, or even you, bully other kids.

You should be very careful and not let this monster scare you.

Do not forget to tell you parents, they will always support you and help you to fight against this monster.

The Send a Photo or Video Monster

This monster always wants you to take pictures or videos of you. He tells you how you should sit for the photos. He also tells you which actions you should do while recording the video. Everything this monster asks from you are things that someone of your age is not supposed to do. Sometimes the "contacting people monster" helps this one, such helper never has good intentions, he is mean and likes stealing pictures from kids to share or sell them to other ugly monsters. He does that to hurt you and make you feel ashamed. He wants to humiliate you.

YOU SHOULD NEVER RECORD OR SEND PICTURES OF ANY PART OF YOUR BODY.

If somebody asks you to do that, tell your parents immediately so that they can handle the situation with the pertinent authority and destroy the monster.

The Dangerous Viral Games or Challenges Monster

This monster usually invites you to do things or play games or challenges that can be dangerous or cause physical pain. These games may make you feel bad because of their results. He will try to fool you saying that you are no longer part of the group and that you will miss your friends. Do not listen to him! Many kids have died because of this monster. Do not take part in these challenges neither follow their instructions.

Remember that true friends take care of each other, enjoy and laugh without blaming. They do not hurt anybody, not even themselves.

We should respect our body, our life and the ones of our, friends, parents, cousins, siblings, and other people.

The Blackmail or Threat Monster

This monster can be very close to you. Sometimes he pretends to be a good friend. He may start pretending to be a good friend to get information and learn from you. When he has already earned your trust, he knows many things that you like. He will use some of your weaknesses to force you to do something that you do not want. When you do something you do not want to, some feelings will come to you that will make you feel sorry and ashamed.

FOR THAT REASON, NEVER DO SOMETHING THAT WILL NOT MAKE YOU FEEL RIGHT; YOU KNOW WHEN SOMETHING IS WRONG.

You have the power to decide what you want and should do. No one should force you to do otherwise. You are worth a lot and you deserve the respect of people, even if you are a child. Do not let the blackmail-threat monster come close to bother you and take control of you.

Internet: A Wonderful Tool

Dear friends, now we want to talk about how wonderful tool Internet is. Because, just as there are bad monsters, there are also things that make our lives easier.

Currently, we can communicate and be in touch with friend sand family members who live far away and whom we cannot visit with frequency. For that purpose, we can use chats, arrange video calls, write emails and be present through social media. Todo our homework, we can do research on the Internet, we can visit libraries and museums, we can have books for free, we can give our opinion freely in blogs or social sites and we can know what others think. Now we also share our likes and interests with many people,and we can learn what is going on in the whole world. Another thing we can do is attend courses and webinars, watch films, listen to music,and watch videos.

We buy in different stores regardless of where they are located and from the comfort of our home. We use electronic mail and that is how we receive and send free messages at any time. All this happens thanks to Internet virtual windows.

And remember, friend, that if you have any doubt about the Internet, you can always turn to your parents or to an adult you trust, who will guide you on how to explore the Internet in a safe way.

THE END

Bibliography:

7 Riesgos de internet para menores
https://www.emy.org/7-riesgos-que-tiene-internet-para-los-ninos

Internet nació de un proyecto militar y hoy es esencial
https://www.elespectador.com/actualidad/internet-nacio-de-un-proyecto-militar-y-hoy-es-parte-esencial-de-la-vida-diaria-article-14119/
Published: May 17, 2008"

Joseph Carl Robnett Licklider." National Academy of Sciences. 1998. Biographical Memoirs: Volume 75. Washington, DC: The National Academies Press. doi: 10.17226/9649.

Joseph Carl Robnett Licklider Wikipedia, The Free Encyclopedia

About the Authors

Patricia Hernández Figueroa (Patty) and Rogelio E. Bernal (Roy) are life partners who have known each other since childhood. He was 14 years old and she was 12 when they first met. Each of them has their own company dedicated to taking care of children at home. For more than 11 years, they have been working with children from 2 months to 12 years of age. Both of them have been awarded different recognition awards for their respective businesses.

Patty holds an Early Childhood Education diploma (ECE) and her business has the Quality Silver Circle certificate, awarded by the State of Illinois. Roy has vast experience in child psychology.

Both have completed different courses and obtained different certifications in Children Development by the Network of Child Care Resource and Referral (INCCRRA).

Currently, in the middle of this pandemic, they were inspired and they joined forces to develop this book and many others with the purpose of explaining complex things to children from 5 to 9 years old.

www.ingramcontent.com/pod-product-compliance
Lightning Source LLC
Chambersburg PA
CBHW040034050426
42453CB00003B/108